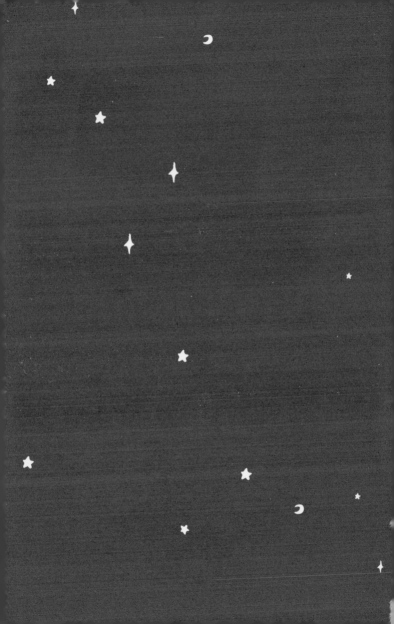

SATURN RETURN
SURVIVAL GUIDE

For my parents, who gave birth
to me during their Saturn Returns.
This book is dedicated to my Pisces
mother, who taught me to dream.
And my Scorpio father, who taught
me how to achieve those dreams.

For everyone out there going
through their Saturn Return – don't
worry, the universe has your back!
You WILL survive and fly high!
You got this!

SATURN RETURN SURVIVAL GUIDE

NAVIGATING THIS COSMIC RITE OF PASSAGE

By Lisa Stardust ✦ Illustrations by Emmy Lupin

Hardie Grant
BOOKS

CONTENTS

INTRO

What do you want to do and, more importantly, who do you want to be when you 'grow up'? Where do you see yourself in the future? And are you ready to take on this new role in life? These are questions we are all faced with once we reach a 'certain age'. In astrology, that time first occurs between the ages of 27 and 29, and it's called the 'Saturn Return'.

Think of the Saturn Return as one's cosmic rite of passage. It's a moment in time when we all begin to reassess our duties, relationships, friendships and role on Earth. It's kind of like a celestial boot camp, in the sense that we are forced to make decisions that will change the course of our lives forever.

The Saturn Return, which happens roughly at ages 27–31, 56–60 and 84–90, is an important time in life, when major restructuring can happen. Career pinnacles or changes, marriages or divorces, and planning one's entrance into cosmic adulthood (whether that means having a child or building an empire) begins. Other meaningful events can also occur, most of which will deeply impact the years that follow.

Because Saturn is a karmic planet, during the Saturn Return we will be learning how to deal with the repercussions of our past actions. Our youthful mistakes may come back to haunt us, and if we have skeletons in the closet, they will most certainly come out to play during this time. Working through trauma can prove to be healing, if you are willing to put the work in. If not, then you will find yourself dealing with the same issues over and over again, on a grander level than before, until you learn your lessons. If you are on the right path, the universe will reward you.

This is a time when dreams can become a reality. Hopes and aspirations can soar. Everything we've wanted to do and achieve is now at our fingertips – if we are open to it. We can create the world we want, and find ourselves along the way. Be open to the opportunities the universe throws your way. In astrology, Saturn is the planet associated with limitations and fears. While this may seem depressing, Saturn brings structure and meaning to our lives. This planet reminds us of our boundaries, our responsibilities and our commitments. Saturn makes us aware of the need for self-control and for boundaries with others. It also defines our personal limits. Saturn is often associated with our fathers or authority figures. In childhood, the discipline, rules and regulations imposed on us by our authority figures, such as parents and teachers, were not always pleasant, but they helped us to understand the world around us. Similarly, Saturn's lessons help us to grow. The Saturn Return gives us a moment to appreciate and reflect on these lessons, and to use them to move forward in our lives.

Now, let's get down to the nitty gritty of your Saturn Return ...

To understand your own personal journey, you'll need to find out what sign your Saturn falls in. You will then need to cast your **birth chart**. Your birth chart is your own personal map to the universe, based on the time, date, location and year in which you were born. Your birth chart can help you unlock the mysteries within, and understand yourself on a deeper level. The chart is divided into 12 different **houses**, each representing a different area of life. You can find a birth chart calculator online.

CHAPTER I

SATURN

The mythology of Saturn

You might be wondering why Saturn is such an austere and karmic planet. Let's do a quick background check on its mythology.

Saturn was one of the twelve Titans, those gods known for their size, strength and immense power until they were deposed by Zeus. Gaia (Mother Earth) and Ouranos (Father Sky) created the first inhabitants of the world – powerful gods who were known for their tough exterior and intense demeanour. Ouranus was not a very proud dad and sought to destroy the 50-headed children by burying them within the Earth. Gaia was infuriated by this and sought help from her other children. Of all her children, only Kronos responded. He waited for his dad and castrated him with a sickle. Kronos became the ruler of the universe after he destroyed his father. He married his sister Rhea and they reigned mightily for a time.

A prophecy said that one of Kronos's kids

would try to depose him, so he decided to swallow them upon birth. But when the sixth child, Zeus, was born, Rhea stole him away to protect him and gave Kronos a stone to swallow instead. Zeus eventually got a job as a cup-bearer to his father, and gave him a poison potion that made him vomit out the swallowed siblings. A major war ensued.

Zeus, ever the cunning warrior, convinced Prometheus (a Titan) to join his team. Kronos and his team of monsters lost. They were banished to the Tartarus, a dark, depressing place at the end of the Earth where Kronos spent eternity reflecting on his actions. Withdrawn from the world, he chose to punish himself for what he had done. In Roman mythology, Kronos became Saturn.

Saturn has several sides, mythologically. Many tend to think of him as an all-round bad guy, but we aim to show you his positive attributes. A king, overcome by a negative state of mind, made the mistake of bad-mouthing Saturn in public court. Saturn, with his perfect timing, just so happened to be flying overhead at that exact moment. Saturn swooped down to greet the king, who panicked and took back his harsh words. But the king's fate was sealed, his karma set. After a series of tormenting experiences, the king lost almost everything. Finally, Saturn reappeared to show mercy and even reward the king for his patience and endurance. He told the king he would grant him anything he wished. Overcome with humility, the king only wished that no-one ever had to endure the kind of suffering he had endured. Saturn was so pleased with the king's wish to save all other beings from suffering that he returned everything he had lost, including his kingdom.

Saturn has a bad rep, and if you choose not to appease him, there can be consequences. In life, just as in the mythic tale, we can learn to use Saturn as a friend rather than a foe.

As you can see, this story applies to the Saturn Return. Saturn has to learn from his mistakes and reap the consequences of his actions – much like you will have to do during this transit. Saturn's lesson is also a karmic one: he was selfish and unkind to others, which led to his demise. He ended up alone because of his decisions. That's not to say that you'll end up in seclusion in the swamps of Earth, but you will find yourself in a place of reflection during this time. You may also find yourself lonely at times, as you are navigating through your life and making important choices that will affect you for years to come.

What role does Saturn play in astrology?

In astrology, Saturn represents limitations and fears. Saturn's placement in an astrology chart and sign can show where problems are in your own life and how you can overcome them. With Saturn, we get what we give, as it's the karmic taskmaster of astrology, rewarding cosmic delights to those who work hard, while causing destruction or breakdowns for those who put minimal effort into achieving their goals. This is a planet that makes lists and ensures that each individual is doing their best to create the life they want. Saturn also represents the relationship we have with our father figures (whereas the Moon represents the maternal influence on us), bosses and people who are in a place of authority over us.

Saturn Retrograde

Planetary slowdowns are called **retrogrades**.
It's quite common for a planet to move
slower than Earth a few times a year while
orbiting the Sun. This doesn't mean the
planet is moving backwards, but the slowness
of its orbit does give us earthlings time to
reflect upon matters. Saturn is a planet that
retrogrades at least once a year. This means
it's quite common for one to have Saturn
Retrograde in their chart. If transiting Saturn
is retrograde while you're having your Saturn
Return, you will find you're being forced to
discuss and analyse personal commitments.
If you are born with Saturn Retrograde in
your **birth chart**, you may decide to assess
relationships and make important changes to
those you hold close to your heart. Marriage
proposals and serious relationships can start
now, or break-ups can occur, depending
on what energy you're working with on a
personal level.

'ALWAYS STAY TRUE TO YOURSELF AND NEVER LET WHAT SOMEBODY ELSE SAYS DISTRACT YOU FROM YOUR GOALS.'

– MICHELLE OBAMA

CHAPTER 2

THE SATURN RETURN

The karmic planet has roughly another 29.5 years until it aligns with the exact degree it was when you were born. This is what's called the Saturn Return. It's an exact conjunction between natal Saturn and transiting Saturn, at the exact degree and sign it was at during the time, date, and year of your birth.

The first Saturn Return

Welcome to the famous astrological 27 club, baby! If you're 27 years old, then Saturn has returned to the **zodiac** sign it was in at the date, time and year of your birth. However, that's just the beginning of the Saturn Return. According to the stars, this is your personal entrance into adulthood. The Saturn Return hits in a person's late twenties, and its impact is felt into their early thirties. During this time, you will undergo many changes and evolve

on a personal level, as you are shedding
everything that doesn't work for you anymore
to become the best version of yourself. Like I
said before, Saturn rewards hard work and
good behaviour – so if you're already living
your best life, prepare to have a wonderful
time. If not, then brace yourself for a bumpy
and wild ride.

Multiple Saturn Returns

Saturn **retrogrades** for four to five months
each year. This means it's common for a
person who's experiencing their Saturn Return
to go through Saturn retrograde two or three
times in a year. What does this mean? It
means that they are being given the cosmic
chance to revise and amend any situations
that need to be fixed. Each time may sting
like a bee, until the person learns what areas
of their lives need changing.

The other Saturn Returns

Given that Saturn comes back to us every 28.5 to 29.5 years, we may experience up to two more planetary returns in our lifetime. The second Saturn Return marks a time of deciding the next phase of life (i.e. retirement) and looking back on all that one's achieved by the age of approximately fifty-eight. The third Saturn Return occurs around the age of eighty-seven. This is a time of reflection, as we note our successes and achievements in life.

CHAPTER 3

FRIEND OR FOE?

Is Saturn a friend or a foe? This is a highly controversial topic among the astrological community.

On one hand, the Saturn Return can bring positive changes. But it can also awaken the parts of us that have been on autopilot, bringing things crashing down as a result. The Saturn Return means we start to see things through a new lens – even if we don't want to. We can't stay out partying late every night, having one-night stands and going to work hungover … can we? Nope. The days of late nights come to an end as we become responsible adults.

The issues come when we start to fight against the notion of adulting ourselves. If we ensure we are acting in a mature fashion, we can avoid the drama and setbacks that notoriously come along with the Saturn Return. Maybe we have a friend who is a bad influence on us and we don't want to cut the cord, even though we are quite aware that we should. In this case, the universe (and by that, I mean Saturn) will come in and end the friendship without warning. Or, if you're in a dead-end relationship and are scared to move on, the cosmos will do its duty and sever ties for you. As long as you look at situations as life experiences and lessons, you will be able to walk away unscathed. Holding on to things that have moved past their expiry date is where the trouble begins. The real theme of the Saturn Return is brutal honesty. Being flexible and recognising that life has other plans for you, ones that you weren't expecting, will help you move forward without any bruises from this celestial adventure. Most importantly, knowing who you are and what you want from life requires you to be real with yourself. Sometimes everything has to fall apart in order to change.

Does this seem overwhelming? It's okay if so. The Saturn Return is an intense time. To keep grounded, please refer to the Saturn Return checklist below to help navigate you through this topsy-turvy time.

1. Breathe.

2. Make a list of who and what are positives in your life.

3. Make a list of who and what are negatives in your life.

4. Decide if you can let go of situations or people who are no longer serving your highest interests (keep in mind this can be a temporary sentiment).

5. Keep breathing.

6. Work with the energy and keep the positives in your life, and implement a boundary with others.

This will help you survive your Saturn Return. Repeat as necessary.

CHAPTER 4

WHAT THE SATURN RETURN MEANS FOR EACH SIGN

Saturn spends two to three years in the same zodiac sign, then moves forward into another sign. It takes on a different role in each sign – Saturn acts in the manner of the zodiac sign and uses the qualities of that sign. For example, Saturn in sparky Aries will be more impulsive than Saturn in pragmatic Capricorn. This helps us see how the planet will act during the Saturn Return. It also tells us what energies it will focus on.

Please refer to your natal Saturn sign, transiting Saturn sign, and sun sign. This will help you understand Saturn's cosmic energy and how it will effect you during your Saturn Return.

Aries

Real talk: Saturn in Aries is this austere planet's least favourite placement. This is because Aries is an impetuous and unstructured sign, and Saturn loves a routine. This placement juxtaposes the sign's and the planet's desires, which are to be free (Aries) and to be bound (Saturn). Aries lack a foundation and understanding of how to stay put in one situation or relationship – they're already moving on to the next best thing. When the Saturn Return occurs, they will be cosmically tasked to stop acting selfishly and learn to put others first – which, as we know, isn't how Aries like to roll. Learning to work cooperatively with others and giving people praise for their efforts will prove to be challenging for the native, as they desperately want to win every competition at all costs. But taking a step back and out of the limelight is necessary. Working with a team of individuals for the same cause will be beneficial for their growth, and sharing the spotlight and trophies will lead to bigger and better successes. The most crucial lesson to be learned is that life isn't a competition. Don't use manipulative tactics to gain notoriety at the office. Working with others will be more fruitful for your advancement.

'You have to be unique and different and shine in your own way.'

– Lady Gaga, *Aries*

Taurus

Saturn in Taurus is a grower, not a shower. When Saturn is in the bullish sign of Taurus the native doesn't like taking chances on who they invest their time and energies with. In fact, they'll spend endless time trying to persuade others to believe in their ideals – even if they are out of touch with the times. Financial security, conservative ideology and sexual insecurities come with having this placement in your **birth chart**. Adapting to different and new sentiments is hard and challenging, as Taureans are extremely set in their ways. Achieving tangible success is always at the front of their minds, as is the quest for material wealth. They are always waiting for their big break or for their ship to come in. During their Saturn Return, Taureans will have a revelation that will offset all of their pre-existing beliefs. They'll find that money isn't all they need in order to have a meaningful life. This change of philosophy will lead them to embrace beauty and the finer things in life (like art and music). Learning to live without financial merit will be taxing; however, they will find that bartering for goods and necessities is more important than a price tag.

'I don't know what else I would be if I wasn't me. I am not looking from the outside, looking back. I am who I am.'

– Cher, Taurus

Gemini

If words could kill, Saturn in Gemini would be serving a life sentence in jail. It's important to note that Gemini is the sign of communication, and on a bad day this native can use harsh sentiments to express their emotions. Saturn isn't known in the cosmos as being nice. In fact, it's known to be grumpy more often than peppy. When Saturn is in Gemini, words can be harsh and communication can be limited, because this placement is not into sharing! In fact, this placement adores rigidity and honesty over tricks and disorganisation. Being scatterbrained won't cut it for Saturn in Gemini, as Geminis put a lot of emphasis on decisive thinking. Learning to organise one's thoughts, beliefs and words will be the core focus during the Saturn Return, along with finding the right way to express one's feelings without being austere. Learning to be less critical and more open to others will be important. The caveat is to give others the same level of sensitivity that is given to the self – to hold others at the same bar we hold ourselves at. Embracing other people's flaws is crucial. After all, no-one is perfect. Give kindness and compassion to others in order to receive it back.

'Imperfection is beauty, madness is genius and it's better to be absolutely ridiculous than absolutely boring.'

– Marilyn Monroe, Gemini

Cancer

This is an erratic placement for Saturn, which is why it's one of its least favourite signs to be in. The Moon, who is the natural **planetary ruler** of Cancer, changes phases and signs every few days, which makes it hard for Saturn to find structure in this sign. Emotions run high, and are often tempestuous and irrational in this placement. This can irritate Saturn, who doesn't really vibe well with displays of emotion. The dichotomy here lies in the native's inability to express their emotions, even though they desperately want to. They will try to implement boundaries with others, but this may not work. During the Saturn Return, they'll come face-to-face with an emotional crisis of sorts, which will make them rethink their value system. Learning to care for others without giving too much of themselves will be the lesson that's learned. Another sentiment that they'll come across will be around giving their hearts freely to others without any selfish attachment aligned with their behaviour. This will be hard, as Saturn in Cancer doesn't like to exist outside its comfort zone – even if it's necessary to do so. Change will come with growing pains, but sometimes pain is essential to learn how to become a more caring and unconditional type of person.

'I'm going to hang out with people,
and I'm going to explore myself,
and I'm okay with that.'

– Selena Gomez, Cancer

Leo

We all know Leos love drama. However, when Saturn aligns with the fiery lion, the need for theatrics is diminished (well, at least for the majority of the time). Saturn brings a sobering element to passionate Leo, who finds glory in excitement and adventure. The upside to this placement is that the native can be a creative force to be reckoned with – but only if they know how to channel their energy productively. The downside is that they can take on a 'woe is me' mentality when they aren't given enough attention. Upon their Saturn Return, they'll have to make tough choices in their lives. In the past they've made their money from artistic and creative ventures, but may now feel uninspired, or unable to find comfort in past endeavours. As a result, they can resort to unscrupulous behaviours to succeed at this time – which will backfire. Taking a creative break from work and life is a great option during this time. Travel the world. Visit museums. Take a course. Focusing the energy inwards will allow Leos to feel reborn with joy, and will motivate them to climb the highest mountains within. They'll learn to give themselves more TLC and to live an honest life.

'You get what you give.
What you put into things is what
you get out of them.'

– Jennifer Lopez, Leo

Virgo

When Saturn is in analytical Virgo, the native has a very discerning palate and attitude towards life. Given that Saturn loves routine, this placement can be rewarding for both the planet and the sign itself. The only issue is that the focus on micro issues supersedes the ability to see the bigger picture. This can lead to obsessive thoughts, which in turn lead to anxiety. The need for perfection is strong, and the native struggles when their life falls short of their high expectations. The flip side is that the native can be quite disorganised with their time and energy before their Saturn Return, which can force them to learn intense lessons during this cosmic transit. It's essential for them to understand that nothing is perfect. This will allow them to stop placing demands upon themselves that are unobtainable. Life is supposed to be messy and not taken too seriously. Letting go of self-doubt and self-criticism will help them see that they can achieve their dreams – they just need to believe in themselves and stop being hard on themselves. A Virgo's biggest critic is always themselves, which is a sentiment they need to mute. If they can learn to let go of fear and judgement, there's nothing they can't achieve.

'I don't like to gamble, but if there's one thing I'm willing to bet on, it's myself.'

– Beyoncé, Virgo

Libra

This is Saturn's favourite placement, as Saturn is exalted in Libra. The native is commitment-oriented. They'll invest a lot of time and thought trying to understand others. The caveat is that they can get too swept away in partnerships – so much so that they forget about their personal needs and desires. Balancing out priorities and responsibilities is important. When this isn't done, it can create issues with others and stress within oneself. During the Saturn Return, it's essential to find structure in work and relationships. Finding friendships and romantic interests that can live up to the native's high expectations is hard, as the 'perfect' person does not exist. Learning to compromise takes a lot of effort and work, but it's essential at this time. Not being too 'extra' and needy with others, and not attracting that type of energy, will lead to a bright future. The same notions apply to finances. It's a great time to start a savings account and learn how to live on a budget. As stated before, structure is essential. Finding a way to live the good life, while still having enough money to pay for rent and groceries is the ultimate challenge – but, with the right advice and planning, this can be attainable.

'I really think a champion is defined not by their wins but by how they can recover when they fall.'

– Serena Williams, Libra

Scorpio

Saturn in Scorpio is intense and insightful. Life has to have meaning and purpose. Superficial relationships and situations never flourish with this placement, as the native is constantly wanting to connect on a deep level. The caveat is that they will only give 100 per cent of their energy to people with whom they see a future (their intuitive spidey senses will alert them to these people). During the Saturn Return in Scorpio, a life choice is made. The native must decide if the path they've been walking down is working or will work for their future selves. Often, a choice is made to veer off the straight and narrow path to take the road less travelled. Allowing themselves to find happiness while embracing the powerful energy that lays within will require time and innate adjustments. After all, they're beginning to see flaws in others reflected in themselves (or vice versa). Leaning into their intuition has been a challenge up until the Saturn Return. During this entrance into celestial adulthood, the native with this placement will quit partnerships and professional endeavours based on their psychic feelings. If it doesn't feel right, then it isn't right. Move on. When the going gets tough, the tough get going.

'Comparisons are easily done once you've had a taste of perfection.'

– Katy Perry, Scorpio

Sagittarius

Saturn in Sagittarius requires the native to be more firm and less fanatical in their thoughts. The archer is a fact-checker and won't take unfounded information with a grain of salt. They are likely to reject high-minded philosophies. At times, they can spread dogmatic sentiments that reflect older testimonials and views. Being a professor at a university or running an online site dedicated to exposing the truth are the two best career choices for this native, as they have the ability to challenge the minds of others. These careers also allow them to find deeper meaning in life and give them the chance to diminish propaganda. Taking risks may be hard, as they'll never bet big or partake in high-stakes gambling, choosing instead to put all of their time and money towards practical matters. Travel may be limited as well, due to fear of leaving home and setting sail to foreign countries. Instead of embracing exotic flavours, they'll prefer bland comfort food. During the Saturn Return, opportunities may arise for the native to travel to foreign places through work, which will give them the chance to see the world. Taking minor risks in life will be necessary – especially when it comes to love and financial investments.

'Just be yourself,
there is no one better.'

– Taylor Swift, *Sagittarius*

Capricorn

Capricorn is one of the two planets ruled by Saturn (the other is Aquarius). Therefore, Saturn in Capricorn is a strong placement for one to have in the **birth chart**, as it focuses on allowing oneself to build strength of character. Yes, at times the native can seem too mature (even acting parental to friends at times). Taking on too much responsibility at an early age will have an effect on the native during the Saturn Return. While they want to boss up, they may experience some setbacks on their path to world domination, because they need to learn to lighten up. Regressing is common, especially if they haven't fully lived out their childhood dreams. However, it's totally possible to embrace both sides of the coin – the need for fun and the drive for success – if balance is found. Here are some words of advice for those going through a Saturn Return with this placement: Don't reach for the stars too fast and soon. Good things come to those who wait. Try to smell the roses now and again as you head up the corporate ladder. Leave time for other desires to manifest in life, apart from professional and monetary gain.

'Don't ever underestimate the impact you can have, because history has shown us that courage can be contagious, and hope can take on a life of its own.'

– *Michelle Obama, Capricorn*

Aquarius

Saturn is at its home when in Aquarius – it's the traditional ruler of Aquarius, so it allows natives with this placement to harness the structure of the karmic taskmaster planet smoothly. When Saturn is in Aquarius in the **birth chart**, it allows this person to take life and humanitarian issues more seriously. The native wants to create a life that's more tailored to their current views, one that also appeals to the overall modern sentiment of the world. The Saturn Return focuses on melding these two worlds together. Upgrading one's views will be challenging at times, especially if they contradict the philosophies of early childhood. Intellectual growth and development will become a core focus of the Saturn Return journey. Letting go of repressed memories may be challenging, as they will come to a head now. But, with the right motivation, the native can purposefully use their past issues as a stepping stone to implement change in society. Adopting a new view will inspire the native to become the unique individual that they desperately want to be. Rebelling against the constraints that hold them back will spark a personal revolution, leading them to advocate for the greater good of others and the underdog.

'Be thankful for what you have; you'll end up having more. If you concentrate on what you don't have, you will never, ever have enough.'

– *Oprah Winfrey, Aquarius*

Pisces

Pisceans often find themselves feeling too guilty or anxious as a result of fear. They shouldn't be scared! Pisceans have the ability to transform their visions into reality, if they allow themselves the opportunity to manifest their dreams. The caveat is that it may be hard to release the insecurities that hold them back from achieving their goals. During their Saturn Return, Pisceans will learn how to swim through their emotions clearly. This means understanding their sentiments on a deeper level. Learning to be more compassionate with themselves and others is key. Just like the waves of the ocean, they will learn to go with the flow. Lighten up! They should feel their feels, but not carry the weight of the world on their shoulders, and embrace their innate artistic gifts to create the world they want. By looking within and being introspective, they have the power to harness their intuition and psychic abilities, and should use these to build the dreams they want. They need to inspire themselves, and let all of the pain and suffering they've felt in their life up until this point become a source of creativity. A great job for Pisceans to choose would be working in art therapy. This will allow them to use their sympathetic sentiments towards helping others.

'Life is very interesting ... in the end,
some of your greatest pains,
become your greatest strengths.'

– Drew Barrymore, Pisces

CHAPTER 5

UNDERSTANDING YOUR BIRTH CHART

Saturn Return in the houses

When interpreting someone's astrological **aspects** and transits, astrologers look to the **birth chart** for guidance. Think of your birth chart as a personal map to understanding yourself.

The birth chart shows our potential – what we want to achieve in this life, what setbacks we will come across, and how to work through them. When we look at Saturn in a birth chart, it's a testimony to our fears, the paternal influence we've encountered growing up, our relationship with authority, the karmic lessons we must learn in this lifetime, and how we can work towards commitment.

Your personal Saturn Return will be in one of the 12 **houses** in a birth chart. It explains what we should be moving towards, and tells us what path will elevate us into greatness and what we need to release during this time.

Aspects are an important part of modern astrology. As the planets move in their elongated orbits around the Sun, they form various angular relationships with one another, using the Sun or Earth as the centre. These are called aspects. The most popular aspects include the conjunction (0 degrees), opposition (180 degrees), trine (120 degrees) and square (90 degrees).

When two planets form an aspect with one another, their energies and natures are said to combine and work either in harmony or in discord. For example, when two planets are exactly on opposite sides of the Sun (or Earth), they are in opposition.

Each of the 12 houses into which the heavens are divided has rulership over specific areas of life.

1st house/ascendant/rising
The house of self and identity

The **ascendant** or rising represents the
sentiments that others notice about you first.
Saturn's position on the **ascendant** can
be a mark of rigidity and sensibility – one
who holds a high bar for themselves and
others. Saturn in the first house shows us
a person who takes life seriously. They are
very relationship-oriented, and are hard on
themselves when partnerships of all kinds do
not work out. Growing up, they had to give
up a part of their childhood due to lack of
parental structure, and were forced to adult
themselves at an early age. During the Saturn
Return, they will find themselves dealing
with resentment towards others, especially
their familial unit, as a result of repressed
sentiments from youth. Finding a healthy
way to release these emotions will require
them to take a look back into their past,
which may be hard to do. The karmic lesson

here is to embrace the child within. Now is the time for these people to treat themselves to all the things they weren't permitted to have as a kid – ditch work for a day at the beach, go to an amusement park with friends, and eat fairy floss for dinner. Staging a revolt from the familial unit and friends will be a part of their Saturn Return, as they're learning to find themselves (and to be a lone wolf while doing so). It's okay to be a black sheep! Becoming the unique individual that they so desperately want to be will require loneliness, solitude and reflection.

2nd house
The house of personal income, self-esteem, and fundamental values

Saturn's placement in the second house can often denote poverty – but not necessarily of the financial kind. While this can mean that the native is having financial setbacks, more often than not it shows that they suffer from low self-esteem, or they have conservative fundamental values that oppose the views of their contemporaries and peers. There's a strong inclination towards rigidity in thinking and finances. This is not a person who speaks their mind freely. They are worried about what other people think, and try to align with the social norms of their family or friends. They also have strong ties to childhood friends and memories, as they tend to have lifelong friends and remain loyal to them at all times. During the Saturn Return, there will be an 'aha' moment for this native. They will deal with self-esteem issues and work towards heightening their inner sentiments and emotions. Learning to love themselves is a lifelong process, but it's the lesson that needs to be learned during the Saturn Return. The relationship with materialism and money will change. Emotional setbacks may happen, but these will be resolved at the end of the Saturn Return. The karmic lesson

is not to place a high value on materialism and wealth, but rather, to place the value on the self. Transforming core beliefs will prove to be hard, as this is the beginning of the evolutionary journey towards confidence and enlightenment.

3rd house
The house of communication, siblings, local travel and early education

The third house represents the spoken and written word, as well as all mercurial things (short-term travel, internet, gossip, news, siblings, and elementary education) – not just on a cerebral level, but on an intellectual and emotional level. When Saturn is in the third house of the **birth chart**, there's a tendency to have a lack of interest in gossip, and for the native to hold honesty in a high regard. The native also doesn't mince words, and uses their social media platform to discuss important matters that affect the world at large. Relationships with siblings may bring conflict, as the native will look to their sibling as an authoritarian figure. When the Saturn Return occurs, the native may be called upon to address issues pertaining to their siblings, resulting in a closer connection.

They will be cosmically tasked to discuss 'the truth' of the matter with their peer group. The native will search for answers that allow them to make decisions about the next phase in life. Secrets will be revealed, which may make them question their childhood. Elementary education and early educational development may bring issues, but the Saturn Return serves to mend them. This is a time for the native to embrace and understand the power their voice and words have. Speaking up is important now. Don't defy the desire to be heard.

4th house
The house of home, personal matters and family

When we see Saturn in the natal fourth house, it points to issues regarding personal security, family and home life, as well as all private matters. There definitely is a defensive attitude in the native here, as they don't like their personal business being aired for everyone to see. This is because as a private person, their sense of security is uprooted by being in the public eye or the talk of the town. Their home will be their sanctuary, but will also create major problems and issues (for example, there may be rusty pipes that require a lot of care, attention and money). There's a strong bond with parental figures, too, who are also a cause of stress for the native. More often than not, the Saturn Return points to issues with both parents, particularly the maternal figure. The mother

will have a strong influence over the native.
Unfortunately, this can indicate that a parent
needs attention due to an illness or other
matter. The Saturn Return in the fourth house
can push the native to purchase a house or
they may inherit property.
The promise of a new chapter in life will
appear now, as moves are being made
towards change.

5th house
The house of creativity, speculative sports, children, romance and casual dating

Have you ever gone on a date with someone who only wanted to talk about world issues, or got deep right away? Chances are, they have Saturn in their fifth house. The native who has Saturn in this house has a reserved nature and longs to be in a serious romantic relationship, but they often find themselves disappointed in love because they have super-high expectations of their partner. They may also be a little reserved when it comes to discussing their sexual turn-ons, as they view sex as a private matter and shy away from topics that they consider taboo. Childbirth may come later in life, or there may be a resistance to having children out of subconscious fears arising from their own childhood trauma. The flip side is that they may have their first born at a young age, but have a complicated pregnancy. Creativity will be a source of annoyance, as they feel artistically locked and challenged. Gambling can create major financial problems throughout life, which is why they resist playing speculative sports. During the Saturn Return, they will make decisions in their life that are related to how and whom they date, what 'type' of person they are attracted to and how to become a more artistically fluid person, and will lean into their sexual inclinations. There will be challenges and obstacles that need to be overcome, particularly their own childhood and adolescent insecurities, before they can have proper relationships and contemplate what being a parent will look like for them. Learning to loosen up and have fun while dating and in life is the lesson to be learned. Reliving their childhood is a must.

6th house
The house of service and daily routine

Saturn finds peace in the sixth house because it can give structure and limits to the daily routines and stresses of our lives. This placement also gives the native peace, knowing that they are working towards a goal that is strengthening their lives and mentality. Keeping up with tasks and having the commitment to see activities through to their fruition requires the strength and determination that Saturn brings. When the Saturn Return occurs here, there's a tendency for the native to be exhausted and to feel stretched thin. They may feel as though the world is against them, and that they don't have any time for self-care.

Because Saturn also represents colleagues and staff (people who work for the native), there may be a shift in the workplace, such as layoffs that minimise the staff, resulting in

the native feeling burdened and overwhelmed
at their job. Relationships with colleagues
can be strained, making one-on-one work
situations tough and tense. If the native is
unemployed, they will need to take time to
look after themselves and create routine,
because a lack of this can cause trouble
in their lives. Without order, they can sleep
all day and will not want to make the
necessary changes in their life. Taking care
of themselves is extra important. Making sure
that their mental and physical health is good
is essential, as it's easy to slip into emotional
downfalls. Being cautious and confident of
their limits will prevent issues along the way.
Most importantly, they need to pay attention
to what their body is telling them.

7th house
The house of all partnerships, relationships and open enemies

Contrary to popular belief, the seventh house is not naturally connected to love. This house shows the type of partnerships we are drawn to. In a **birth chart**, Saturn in the seventh house may mean a number of things. It can mean an early or late marriage, that the native enjoys the company of 'Saturnian' or older people, or that the native has a distant approach to partnerships and/or is attracted to those who have a colder, more reserved personality. During the Saturn Return, the native may find that the lesson they are dealing with is related to how and to whom they commit. This doesn't have to be romantic. It can simply be that they overextend themselves for others, or promise too much of their time, only to learn that they have to be pragmatic and responsible

about their limitations. The other side of this aspect can show that the native takes relationships very seriously – to the extent that they don't want to be around anyone who diminishes their public standing or ridicules their level of commitment. These individuals really want to be good partners, and to do this means that they must be upfront about their limits and needs. This will not only benefit them, but also their partner. The flip side is that they may experience karmic repercussions from a former relationship. If they were nice to someone they dated or aligned with in the past, they'll be rewarded pleasantly. If not, havoc may take place, causing break-ups and shake-ups to ensue, with the individual learning a heartbreaking lesson in the end.

8th house
The house of sex, death, other people's money, and transformation

Saturn in the eighth house represents apprehension in growth. This placement can indicate many things, but mostly it shows the native's hesitance when it comes to personal evolution. In fact, they may find any circumstance that makes them shift beyond their current situation to be tedious and frustrating. There are also issues with joint finances, as the native may be attracted to people who have financial issues or are in debt. There's a fear when it comes to accumulating debt of any kind, which will make this person anxious and fearful of unpaid bills, meaning they will pay their bills right away. It's common for the native to be miserly and ask for money (even if they have enough to get them by), as they may see their pockets as always being empty when in fact they aren't. During the Saturn Return, situations may occur that require immediate action. This will push the native to transform and blossom into the person they want to be but are afraid to become, which will be challenging. Karmic lessons will hit them hard, as they are learning that without flexibility and growth, matters can and will come to a head. Regarding finances, there will be major lessons on how to handle credit card payments and loans properly. Learning to live on a budget and not wanting to spend beyond their means is important. On the flip side, the native may receive an inheritance that will boost their bank account and financial wellbeing.

9th house
The house of philosophy, long-distance travel and higher education

Saturn in the ninth house represents an individual who is practically minded and spends a lot of time intellectualising about society. This native is unlikely to take flights of fancy and risks when it comes to life – especially their education. The only issue is that they may be closed-minded and not open to hearing opposing philosophies. The native will enjoy and strive in higher education, even prolonging their tertiary studies, meaning they will commit fully to higher education. There's a reluctance to undertake long-distance travel, because the native will find solace in their local community and will not want to go overseas if this is not necessary. During the Saturn Return, the native may decide to go back to university to undertake a degree in a subject that they wish to pursue professionally in the long term. This will juxtapose with their former studies and inner philosophies. They are open to evolving and questioning their beliefs in order to become an educated individual. There will also be a need to travel overseas in order to understand different cultures. The caveat is that this trip may not happen or may not be as much fun as they had hoped, which will keep them stuck in their local communities indefinitely. Connecting to their core beliefs will be a long process; however, the Saturn Return will inspire and motivate them to unite with their fundamental values on a deeper level than ever before.

10th house
The house of public image and career

The native with this placement finds their
career calling at an early age. They are
drawn at a young age to leadership roles
and, as a result, their professional goals may
include being the boss of everyone – even
the world. When only young, this person will
consider taking on jobs that require a lot of
effort and personal resources, but in time
they will find that being in charge isn't all it's
cracked up to be. In fact, it limits the amount
of fun they can have, because it means they
are required to be responsible at all times.
Upon the Saturn Return, these individuals will
question their professional motives and their
relationship with authority. Only choosing to
work for companies that they have a future
with will make them feel as though they are
on the road to success. However, they will
have to decide if they want to compromise
their values for fame and acclaim, or swallow

their pride and accept that their inner
philosophies and ideals do not matter.
This may create conflict within the native,
calling for a new career path or direction.
They may also experience a karmic
awakening, in which they opt to take on a
lower position at their dream job in order
to build the future they want. One thing is
certain – they will make major changes that
will affect the rest of their lives.

11th house
The house of friendships, goals and humanitarianism

Real talk: This native enjoys being a social
butterfly, but they don't like belonging to
too many groups. This can make friendships
seem like a burden at times, as they prefer to
be a lone wolf – superficial relationships need
not apply. Only friendships with people who
converse about important matters matter
to this native. Another sentiment of this

Saturnian placement is that the native will
find solace in committing to humanitarian
endeavours that help others. The caveat is
that they do not want to work with their peers
on helping the world. Instead, they opt to
be leaders in their own light by working solo
and directly with charities. In addition, they
don't publicly announce their donations or
the causes that they give time and money to.
During the Saturn Return, we can expect this
native to get fed up with the superficialities
of their friendships and find a new crew to
hang with. They may also decide to change
their life path and dedicate themselves fully
to charitable causes, such as starting work
with a not-for-profit organisation or using
their social media platforms to promote
humanitarianism. The only issue that they
will encounter is an inner reluctance to sever
ties with some friends or individuals who are
a bad influence, due to their desire to believe
the best in others – even if they've been

proven wrong by those individuals.
This is because it's hard for them to connect
with their peers, and severing relationships
is hard because they don't like to let go of
relationships that are toxic or unhealthy.

12th house
The house of clandestine situations or imprisonment

Saturn is very happy in the 12th house. This
is because Saturn, who is the karmic teacher
of the **zodiac**, is able to punish these natives,
and force them to take responsibility for
their actions. The caveat is that they may
feel so much guilt for their indiscretions that
this brings on depression or causes them to
self-harm. The flip side to this natal aspect
is that the native may be drawn to secret
relationships or affairs that stem from their
insecurities. Their confidence may not be
high, which will lead them to be involved with
partners who don't see them clearly or do

not have their best interests at heart. During the Saturn Return, the native will have to reassess their relationship with the paternal or authoritative figure in their life in order to understand their relationship patterns, while also dealing with personal trauma. Healing can happen, but only if the native is ready to release pain and anger. This will require a deep dive into their emotional side, which can prove challenging. Understanding their relationship with drugs and alcohol during the Saturn Return will also create deeper conscious clarity within, and will help to curb such cravings. The native may even realise the connection between mental problems and their family, helping them recognise a pattern that is consistent in all their family members, including themselves. Working in solitude will have its perks too, but isn't necessarily something they will feel comfortable committing to, because isolation will prove to be lonely and challenging.

Saturn and other planets

We can explore the Saturn Return story further by understanding its connection to the planets in our **birth charts**. If you take a deeper look at your birth chart, you may find that Saturn connects with other planets. If it does, then you will also be affected by the energies of those planets during your Saturn Return.

Generational planets

Generational or outer planets (like Uranus, Neptune and Pluto) move slower than planets like the Sun, Mars, Mercury, the Moon, Venus, Saturn, and Jupiter. They are called generational planets because their transits span from 7-13 years, defining a whole generation of people.

The Sun

The Sun represents one's vitality and will

The Sun astrologically represents one's purpose and motivation. Therefore, the Saturn Return can bring a plethora of challenges if the individual's actual life direction is not being completely fulfilled. Those who have planetary connections to their own Sun sign through their Saturn Return may feel this more heavily than others. For example, an alignment between Saturn and the Sun would bring on a time to be taken seriously in all aspects of life, especially in work matters and relationships. This would be quite similar, but with a lighter tone, through a sextile or trine aspect. It is felt more heavily via a square and can even indicate some kind of loss of a boss or paternal figure, and certain identity struggles in general. Your solar power in astrology is literally your life force shining through, giving you a sense of direction and innate understanding, but it's also about finding your own light in this lifetime. The Saturn Return's job is to help you find this inner light more deeply, while also rebuilding your personal understanding of who you are and why you came to this planet at this particular time. It can mean deconstructing some pretty powerful boundaries that have been set up through your ego. What you thought you were supposed to do or who you were supposed to become is based on your hard work and dedication through this transit, which heeds your rite of passage on the wheel of karma. How this transit will leave an individual changed is quite personal for every sun sign. In general, **fire signs** are working on their role of being more active in society; **earth signs** are learning how to stand their ground and be solid in themselves; **air signs** are learning how to be extremely clear about what they want; and **water signs** are learning how to go with the flow of life's many ups and downs.

The Moon
The Moon represents emotions, the maternal and our memories

The Saturn Return can influence your Moon sign quite brilliantly if you step away from personal fears and let its impact become something undeniable. If the Saturn Return occurs when the Moon is also in your birth sign, this can be an extremely crucial lesson around home, family and emotional health. Often this is linked to a combination of those inherited **aspects** of the maternal and paternal line if directly aspected through a conjunction, or even a square. Overcoming certain obstacles and stigmas around mental health are a major contributor towards personal understanding. This would be more easily overcome via a sextile or trine, but would also require careful attention and personal work as well. The hard lunar aspect to Saturn can bring on a crisis around uncovering which emotions are actually

owned by the person themselves and which emotions were projected onto them as children. This is not an aspect for the faint of heart by any means, and can sometimes require those with personal placements to step away from outdated doctrines that were once seen as law in their lives. The moon sign is highly influenced at one's emotional core through your Saturn Return. You might need to make some emotional adjustments and sort out your own personal commitments. Overall, it's going to bring you a sense of individuality and personal power that you may not have felt before. The idea is to let go of what is expected of you and truly connect with what your intuitive self is instructing you to do on a soul level.

Mercury

Mercury represents travel, communication, siblings and information

The influence of Saturn with cognitive Mercury can be a little tricky during the shift of a Saturn Return. This can be a very serious transit, where even the most jovial of personalities can seem more sullen and pensive. A conjunction can indicate a sudden life event that completely changes one's mind, and hence one's own life path. This can be seen in someone who wakes up one day and changes their career on the spot, as a result of either a dream or occurrence that shows them a brand new way of thinking. A trine or sextile would signal a more gradual process, and might even enhance the individual's current standing in their path of professional pursuits. A square can indicate certain difficulties around their career, siblings and neighbours. There is a mental cloud that can form if the native doesn't

understand what is wrong and is foggy
about what needs to be changed. Issues
around their mental habits can surface, and
a feeling of being stuck in the past or needing
to revisit something that was left behind. In
general, looking towards your inner voice
for knowledge and enlightenment can also
set you on a track towards learning new
things that were once seen as off limits. This
can bring on a new skill set that hasn't even
been considered prior to your Saturn Return,
and can lead you down a path of rewarding
self-discovery. This is why many find their
actual profession later in life, as this transit
appreciates the importance of gaining
knowledge through life experiences that are
inherently linked to maturity.

Venus
Venus represents affection, artistry, money and sensuality

Devotion is a major aspect of love when it comes to the Saturn Return. Venus, being the planet of your heart chakra, brings some very healing vibrational forces if you look at the bigger picture. This aspect can feel heavy at times, or even like a wet towel if you've been looking only for flirtatious fun. A direct conjunction between Venus and Saturn can feel like a hefty burden on your spirit, but it can also be the glue that binds you to your soulmate, leading you down a long road with the partner you've always wanted. Saturn and Venus **aspects** can absolutely influence marriages and those relationships that are in it for the long haul. This includes the harmonious sextile and trine aspects as well, which would allow for more freedom in general. The square would be felt, and could possibly indicate a reversal of certain romantic scenarios during the passage of one's Saturn Return. Many are going to be challenged when it comes to their ideals surrounding love, self-worth and financial security. Wealth can be accumulated during this cycle, as the individual is coming of age and is being directly confronted by their long-term spending habits. Because Saturn always prefers us to learn through experience, this can also indicate a difficult situation surrounding money, and romance can be the source of the lesson during this period. It's always the tough love transits that let us all know how much we can take and what really makes us who we are in the end. Relationships that start during or as a result of a Saturn Return will be ones that you will always refer back to as your greatest teacher, helping you identify what you truly want in life.

Mars
Mars represents action, arguments and warfare

When it comes to your Saturn Return, work is extremely important, and Mars brings on the action! The factors that influence this energy really get into the nitty gritty of your personal chart, as the connection between Mars and Saturn can also indicate leaving certain abusive behaviours behind. This is where personal maturity and self-awareness need to be taken to the highest level, as Saturn requires thoughtful actions and a need to redo or reform any impulsive errors of the past. For instance, if this is aspected via a conjunction, this can test your leadership skills in some capacity. Whether or not you are mentally ready has nothing to do with this. The square can be more challenging, as this involves competing personalities and you will have to set your personal opinions to the side. The sextile and trine would be more inclusive, and might even involve a team effort that is highly rewarding, helping you to see your true star power. Overall, Saturn wants you to take care of your physical self if this planet is in your sign. This can bring a huge shift in your overall exercise routines, and nutritional habits that sculpt a new way of being. You are being asked to dedicate more time to yourself if you've been neglecting your body in any way. For some this can also be connected to therapeutic modalities that also help them to release any pain or trauma from the past.

Jupiter
Jupiter represents expansion, luck,
philosophy and higher education

The connection of your Saturn Return with
Jupiter is a generational aspect and will be
felt as a certain collective ideal. Jupiter's
representation of luck, abundance, marriage,
and even spiritual gratitude is going to be
seen through world events. The influence of
a Saturn Return conjunct Jupiter is highly
auspicious, presenting major movements
in the current structure of society that can
ultimately shift the way things are going on a
personal level. Being able to adjust to what is
going on around you can help, and as Jupiter
is a highly expansive planet, this can also
be sorted out through even the toughest of
squares. A sextile or trine would be delightful,
bringing you satisfaction and great success.
Jupiter adds quality to your chart, and
Saturn wants you to feel the structure and
benefits of your diligence. During your

Saturn Return this planetary connection marks a mere checkpoint of your own behaviours. Are you overdoing life in certain respects and indulgences, or are you staying the course? There's a reward for those who are not trying to take the easy way through, and you will see the tangible benefits in various capacities. This can also include the influence of a binding marriage to something or someone. Spirituality plays a major role here, as your mind is expanding to the greater possibilities out there in the universe, while also remaining practical through Saturn's more down-to-earth approach.

Generational influences

Saturn conjunct Jupiter:
1961, 1980, 2000, 2020, 2040

Saturn square Jupiter:
2016, 2024/2025, 2035/2036

Saturn trine Jupiter:
2013, 2014, 2026, 2027, 2034

Saturn
***Saturn represents limits, structure,
boundaries, authority and the paternal***

The influence of your Saturn Return is in fact
the transit conjunction of Saturn to your
personal Saturn, as this planet takes about
27 to 30 years to cycle the entire **zodiac**
and thus return to your own natal point in
your astrology chart. This is a time of coming
into your own, and being given a torch of
knowledge from the universe. You are finding
your way through the world, and through
extreme dedication and perseverance, can
truly become the success you set out to be.
This is one of the most challenging times – a
period that simultaneously deconstructs
old ways of thinking while building you up
to understanding your life purpose. You
experience certain **aspects** to your natal
Saturn throughout your life, known as squares
and oppositions, which occur every seven
years or so and also aid in upgrading your

current path of influence. For example, Saturn opposition is first experienced around the ages of 13 to 17, where one begins to challenge authority around them and to discover what makes them authentically themselves. It's experienced again between the ages 40 to 44. As Saturn cycles throughout your life, even after your Saturn Return, you'll also experience the lesson of commitment through various life events. The Saturn Return transit wants to bring you major responsibility in your overall life. Professional and business matters are major players in this area, but this is not limited to your career. The path of your karmic duty is going to require you to defy all odds. This is an ultimate test of what you want versus what is expected of you based on your upbringing. It's absolutely up to you to decide what you are ready to work through, and what Saturn knows you're ready to handle. This can be a heavy transit, as things can feel like they go from one extreme to the other.

Uranus
Uranus represents change, revolutions and rebellions

The planet Uranus can add a little chaos to Saturn's overall need for security. As a generational influence, Uranus has no interest in going with the status quo. In fact, this energy is the antithesis of any strict authoritative influences. The conjunction of Saturn and Uranus can add both brilliance and immediate destruction to old methods of approach. This can even be a war or revolutionary aspect overall. The influence of a square or opposition causes friction between one's need to rebel and the systems that bind. A more helpful sextile or trine can also lead to major societal epiphanies by creating cultural shifts and rebellions. Uranus, known as 'The Great Awakener', is at odds when it aligns with authoritative Saturn. This is a time of radical changes in thinking among the collective (Uranus) that opposes the views of the government (Saturn). Revolutions and rebellions can occur on a societal level. On a personal level this is felt by going against the grain. During your Saturn Return this will bring the shocking realisation that the 'adults' around you are actually not doing their job well. This is a huge wake-up call, especially if you've been feeling left out or even considered an outcast in various social circles. This may result in you stepping away from a family or role that has a very conservative outlook on life, or have even been entering a realm of work that is more socially aware. Ultimately, Uranus wants you to step up to the negative laws that Saturn has been enforcing, which requires extreme bravery and independence.

Generational influences

Saturn conjunct Uranus:
1942, 1988, 2032

Saturn opposite Uranus:
1965, 1966, 1967, 2008/2009, 2010,
2056/2057

Saturn square Uranus:
1999/2000, 2021, 2043

Saturn trine Uranus:
2016/2017, 2047/2048

Neptune
Neptune represents fear, illusion,
creativity, decay, sentimentality and
dreaminess

This aspect in the sky between outer
planets Neptune and Saturn can be quite
nebulous. Neptune's influence on your
Saturn Return can dissolve certain realms of
understanding, and even lead to particular
ideological perspectives being incorporated

into the governing structures of society.
As a result, some generations may have a
strong focus on incorporating or dissolving
various religious connections in their own
governmental systems. For example, when
Neptune aligns with your Saturn Return it
may be necessary to combine both spiritual
practices and career-related pursuits into
one unit. You may feel it is imperative to have
both elements actively working in your life in
order for things to make sense to you. This is
more interesting with a square or opposition,
as personal illusions are being dissolved
while you are meeting life's hardships. A
generation can experience great strife and
discontent, as there is a particular mentality
captured in the framework of institutionalised
support systems. While a sextile or trine can
be more inspirational overall, this can also
require incredible dedication and wisdom.
What your personal natal Neptune wants
you to understand during a Saturn Return is

that you are not alone in the universe. The
idea is to surrender to your higher power and
appreciate the challenge that Saturn brings
to you as both a lesson and a gift. This is a
vote of confidence from your spirit guides and
ancestors, who only want the best for you.

Generational influences

Saturn conjunct Neptune:
1952/1953, 1989, 2026

Saturn opposite Neptune:
1972/1972, 2006/2007, 2042/2043

Saturn square Neptune:
2015/2016, 2033/2034

Saturn trine /Neptune:
2001/2002, 2012/2013, 2036/2037, 2049

Pluto

Pluto represents unexpected transformation and evolution

The influence of Saturn and Pluto is one of the most magnetic transits to experience. Both planets are power players in the heavens, and when they align they pack an incredible punch. During your Saturn Return you are generally analysing your connection to outer authority, while also taking personal assessments for yourself on a highly karmic scale. As Saturn requires you to be accountable for who you are and what you've been involved in thus far, this also brings forward the aspect of being answerable for your actions and behaviours in life. If there is some piece of yourself that needs to be changed, this is the time to do it. Certain generations will experience this innately as a collective unit. For example, a highly transformative conjunction between Saturn and Pluto makes major waves and sets a path of exponential enlightenment that is

undeniable, not only for the individual, but
also for systems that involve any form of
abuse of power. An opposition would create
a more mirrored approach to this ideal, while
a square would be felt more heavily through
forceful actions. A sextile or trine to this
energy brings on a feeling of hope in general,
but requires the individual to keep an open
mind and not get caught up in the potential
energy. Either sextile or trine, the influence
of Pluto in your chart during a Saturn Return
means that change is inevitable, and leads
you through your own cycle of rebirth.

Generational influences

Saturn conjunct Pluto:
1947, 1982, 2020, 2053

Saturn opposite Pluto:
1965/1966, 2001/2002, 2035/2036

Saturn square Pluto:
1955/1956, 1973/1974, 1993/1994,
2009/2010, 2028/2029

North Node of Destiny

The North Node of Destiny represents one's fate in this lifetime

The North Node of Destiny is a beautiful aspect in general, as you are uncovering your personal life path through fated events of this spiritual alignment. Having this node in an aspect during the Saturn Return, a true commitment is embodied and unfolded through this destined path pulling you in the direction you need to go. This can feel uncomfortable for many, as this is a new way of life, and is very much not what you are used to doing. Because Saturn Returns reflect your purpose overall, this can mean you have to step entirely out of the box and create something off the beaten track for yourself. This can include opening up a business of your own, or being more visible in a way that you had not previously thought possible. In general, the nodes have a strong feeling of being in the right place at the right

time. They can bring on meetings that lead
to deeply connected relationships, and even
attract your soulmate. Pay careful attention
to those intuitive hunches you get – you are
being guided by the universe and led towards
those paths that magnetically align you with
the person you came here to become. This
is experienced in all **aspects** and transits to
your nodes, including a conjunction, and is
just as encouraging with a square as well.

South Node of Destiny
*The South Node of Destiny represents our
past-life duties*

The South Node represents your past life
and what needs to be purged away. During
your Saturn Return an aspect to this point
is considered a very lucky placement, as
it means one enters a karmic commitment
overall. You can literally pull in people, places
and experiences that were part of your overall
genetic imprint and remind you why you

signed up for this job of being you in the first place. This is an extremely fated role at this time in your life. This can play out through some difficult personalities that test your patience on a daily basis, but it can also make you into an undeniable presence in numerous walks of life. It can also lead to certain lucky breaks for you, and set you up with an amazing mentor who is here to show you the ropes. Success is best achieved by showing respect to the authority figures around you, and by being aware of those relationships that no longer serve you on a spiritual level. This brings out your inner determination, and even gets you in touch with your inner healing powers. However, there is always give and take with any South Node aspect, as you are now required to allow for certain unhealthy and addictive qualities to fall away. This is where you are faced with your shadow side, and are supported by Saturn to reconstruct into the highest version of yourself.

Romance
The houses

When it comes to romance, we look to the first house in the **birth chart** to see one's overall vibe, the fifth house for casual dating and the seventh house for intimate relationships. Usually, when the Saturn Return falls on the **ascendant**/first house, it shows that the native is in the mood to be in a serious relationship because they feel that's an important part of adulthood. When the Saturn Return is in the fifth house, it makes the native want to connect with someone on a deeper level. However, it can also dampen their dating lives because they can be a little too picky about who they hang with. The Saturn Return in the seventh house indicates a desire to commit to another – even if the person isn't necessarily compatible with them. It also will bring the current karmic lessons regarding love. What goes around comes around in romance here.

Planets

Venus is the planet of love and money. When the Saturn Return falls upon Venus, we can assume that love and relationships will be affected the most. The Saturn Return and Venus, when together, make us want to commit on a more intimate level. However, the road to relationship bliss is paved with hardships, as Venus doesn't want to work for affection and Saturn makes us put effort into procuring such emotions. Therefore, it can make attaining love a little harder – but it's totally worth the effort.

Family

The houses

In the **birth chart**, the fourth house represents family and home life. When the Saturn Return falls in this house of the birth chart, there's a need to define boundaries within the family. This usually occurs with the paternal figure. It can also mean that issues from childhood have a chance of being repaired.

Planets

The Moon represents our personal feelings and is associated with the maternal. When the Saturn Return aligns with the Moon, there's a chance to revisit and heal childhood trauma. It also discusses how you would like to parent yourself and another. Issues with the mother can turn around if both parties are willing to repair the relationship.

Career

During the Saturn Return in the 10th house, there's a tendency to re-evaluate one's career. Are we happy with the way things are going? Do we enjoy our profession? There's often a career switch during the Saturn Return in the 10th house, because the native decides on a new path for themselves.

Self-care and empowerment

Venus is associated with self-care and
empowerment – because if we feel good,
our self-esteem can soar. The caveat is that
it may be challenging to feel good with
this combo, which can lead to anxieties.
Routine workouts, healing baths and
daily affirmations can all help boost one's
confidence and lead one towards greatness.

Saturn aspects

Aspects in astrology show how planets
connect. The Saturn Return serves a prolific
role that will give us insight into what we
will need to work on during this time. It's not
uncommon for the same people, situations
and themes to reappear during the times that
aspects occur.

The only two major transits that bring
matters to a head are the Saturn square and
Saturn opposition. These **'hard' aspects**

awaken our charts and serve as a great source of insight into how we are moving towards and working with the Saturn Return energy.

The Saturn square (Saturn squaring transiting Saturn)

Think of this as your pre- and post-Saturn Return check-in. A square in astrology occurs when **zodiac** signs are at a 90-degree angle to each other. This is a wake-up call to take action and make clear decisions. Usually, this happens every seven years. It's the universe's way of making sure we are doing the work we need to do to ensure we are living our best lives. Don't forget, Saturn is the karmic taskmaster and teacher, so it's important that it checks in every once in a while to give us a nudge in the right direction (if we are on the wrong path), or to commend us on our hard efforts towards soulful evolution.

Signs that square each other:

Aries squares Cancer and Capricorn

Taurus squares Leo and Aquarius

Gemini squares Virgo and Pisces

Cancer squares Libra and Aries

Leo squares Taurus and Scorpio

Virgo squares Gemini and Sagittarius

Libra squares Cancer and Capricorn

Scorpio squares Leo and Aquarius

Sagittarius squares Virgo and Pisces

Capricorn squares Aries and Libra

Aquarius squares Taurus and Scorpio

Pisces squares Gemini and Sagittarius

The Saturn opposition (Saturn opposing transiting Saturn)

The Saturn opposition occurs when natal Saturn opposes signs with transiting Saturn in an **orb** of 180 degrees to each other.

The first one occurs at 15 years of age and the second one occurs at the age of 44 to 45. This transit starts, and reawakens, the story of the Saturn Return (the same story and all the key players will be involved in this transit). There may be a smidge of regret in our life and actions, as we come to clearly see that we are not living up to our potential or our dreams. Situations and relationships will transform due to the foundation crumbling if it's not strong.

Opposing signs

Aries – Libra

Taurus – Scorpio

Gemini – Sagittarius

Cancer – Capricorn

Leo – Aquarius

Virgo – Pisces

'THE ONLY WAY TO
DO GREAT WORK IS
TO LOVE WHAT YOU DO.
IF YOU HAVEN'T FOUND
IT YET, KEEP LOOKING.
DON'T SETTLE. AS WITH
ALL MATTERS OF THE
HEART, YOU'LL KNOW
WHEN YOU FIND IT.'

– STEVE JOBS

CHAPTER 6

ASTROLOGICAL TIPS TO HELP YOU SURVIVE THE SATURN RETURN

During the Saturn Return, you'll find that your emotions are in flux – especially during planetary retrogrades (Saturn in particular). Allow yourself time to figure it out. Don't rush the process of growing.

At the end of the day, you're going to survive this transit. All that's really left to do is just sit back, relax and enjoy the ride that is coming your way. Yes, it is going to be all kinds of weird, wonderful and uncomfortable, all at the same time. But it will also be the most satisfying time of your life. You're becoming an adult, according to astrology. Embrace these growing pains and step up! Go with the flow!

Manifestations

Manifestation allows us to bring and see our truest desires. Through this technique, we can create the world we want. By being clear about one's intention, you can ask the proper questions within or to the universe. This will help you to draw in the right intentions. By being honest with ourselves, we can get to the underlying objectives quickly and concisely, without hesitation.

Manifestation 101

Think of something that you would like to experience, to know, and to be – something that is important and meaningful to you and that you desire strongly. Focus on this now. See yourself having this energy in the best possible way. Take a few moments to visualise this desire already existing in the present. Feel the emotions that accompany this desire. Does this desire feel exciting?

(If not, think of a desire that elicits excitement
and that feels energising and expansive when
you imagine having it.) This tool will help
you attract the passions you want during
the Saturn Return. Using the information
from your **birth chart**, such as Saturn's
placement, the sign Saturn resides in, etc.,
you can find the best idea to manifest for
yourself.

Remember when you mapped out your
birth chart and found the placement for
Saturn in the **houses**? Now you can use
that information to find out what your soul's
purpose is according to your personal birth
chart. Just like the planet Saturn, things
come full circle now.

Here are some helpful ideas.

1st house

Understanding the relationship with yourself
through interactions with others will force
you to reconsider one-on-one connections.
Therefore, it's important to meditate on the
type of relationships you want with others.

2nd house

Financial opportunities may prove fruitless.
The lesson is to take control of your bank
account and make long-term investments that
seem right for you. Manifesting monetary
growth is key.

3rd house

The relationship you have with your siblings
and honesty can evolve now. Learn to speak
your truth through soulful connections and
meditation with the self. Talk therapy is
favoured here, for healing.

4th house

Home and family life will become important now – even a source of stress. Using protection magic against negative elements will clear the space and mind from pessimistic energy.

5th house

With Saturn limiting the house of fun and creativity, it's a call for you to embrace your inner child – you know, the younger version of yourself who felt stifled. Now you can let your sweet child out and do all the things you wished you could do in your youth.

6th house

A regiment may be needed to provide structure, but you can manifest good health this way. Stick to a routine, just don't be hard on yourself if you can't keep up with it every day. Manifest self-care, with the long-term goal of sticking to it.

7th house

It's time you made a list of who your ideal partner is. You can be as nitpicky as you like. After all, you are defining what you want from love and commitment. When you are done making your list about your dream partner, you may find you have conjured them – they may soon appear in real life.

8th house

Manifest the idea of living a debt-free life, one without the constraints of owing other people money. Then you can figure out ways to maintain your finances on your own two feet.

9th house

Expanding your mind may be hard, but opening yourself up to opportunities will prove to be fruitful. You can use your knowledge to manifest a new perspective on life.

10th house

If you're looking for a new job, this is your time to make a move. A road opener spell (like the one below) will help you find opportunities. In fact, they will come to you as a result of working your magic, which will help you find the right career path.

11th house

Friends may come and go, but the ones who are worth their weight in gold will remain by your side. Find yourself in the group and manifest longevity with your squad through humanitarian projects.

12th house

Dealing with past pain and trauma is essential. Be honest with yourself about your circumstances. Don't be shy and hide away from yourself. Look yourself directly in the mirror and practise daily affirmations to boost your confidence.

Planetary connections

Here's how Saturn vibes with the planets (both personal and transiting ones) during your Saturn Return.

The Sun
Focus on your ego and vitality. Don't let people dim your shine and brightness.

The Moon
Understand your feelings. Stop gaslighting yourself and others. Connect with your mother.

Mercury
Words have power. Assert yourself and use your voice to make change.

Venus
Maintaining love and money takes a lot of work. Don't let that stand in the way of understanding your greatness.

Jupiter

Being stuck can be hard, but you will move past uncertainty in no time. Stay the course!

Mars

Stop fighting against a lost cause. Use your energy and pick your battles wisely. Don't be a bully or allow yourself to be bullied by others.

Saturn

AKA the Saturn Return. Find your path in life by being honest with yourself, and make your own choices – ones that will lead you towards happiness.

Uranus

Rebelling against authority and the status quo will push you to your highest potential. You can soar to new heights if you revolt against the norm.

Neptune

Let go of fear. Find your strengths by listening to your dreams and by opening yourself up to the unknown.

Pluto

This is a time of evolution and change – life will never be the same. You have the power to rule over your Saturn Return and the world.

The North Node of Destiny

Contemplate on who and what you want to commit to now.

The South Node of Destiny

Let go of old connections that no longer serve your highest purpose.

'YOU CAN'T JUST SIT THERE AND WAIT FOR PEOPLE TO GIVE YOU THAT GOLDEN DREAM. YOU'VE GOT TO GET OUT THERE AND MAKE IT HAPPEN FOR YOURSELF.'

– DIANA ROSS

CHAPTER 7

MAGICAL TIPS TO HELP YOU SURVIVE THE SATURN RETURN

Now that you've noted which parts of your birth chart you can use to help you towards manifesting your proper visions, the magical tips provided by contributors in this chapter will help you use the forces of the universe to aid, protect and propel you towards living your best life during your Saturn Return.

Tarot magic – by Sarah Potter

Sarah Potter is a New York-based tarot reader, colour magic practitioner and curator

The Saturn Return can be a challenging time in one's life, as it represents a passage of time where we are asked to ascend and 'grow up' into our next phase of life. Saturn is the cosmic disciplinarian, who pushes us with obstacles and challenges that bring us greater strength and wisdom. As we navigate this challenging time, tarot proves to be a supportive and effective ally.

In tarot, Saturn is represented by The World, the final card in the Major Arcana, ending the Fool's Journey before starting over and beginning again with newfound wisdom and experiences. In the Rider Waite Tarot deck, illustrated by Pamela Colman Smith, the World card is depicted by a central figure, a dancer clad in only a scarf and encircled by a wreath. The four corners showcase a man, a bull, a lion and an eagle, symbolising the four **cardinal** directions as well as the four **fixed signs** of the **zodiac**. The composition of this card shows balance and harmony, coinciding with the overall meaning of The World. This is the feeling of accomplishment that comes with the completion of any cycle, and it's the summation of the triumph of moving through the fears and anxieties brought up in the Saturn Return.

Use these three tarot spreads to offer wisdom and a new perspective on your current situation. In order to do each spread, create a quiet sanctuary for yourself and your cards. Take a few deep breaths, close your eyes, and give the deck a good shuffle.

An overall Saturn Return lesson spread

Are you feeling completely lost about how to navigate your Saturn Return? This five-card spread will help you uncover the lessons you need to focus on so you can move forward through this current cycle.

The first card reveals the main theme of your Saturn Return. This is the current energy you will experience during this time. The second card points to a major lesson you will learn through your Saturn Return. This lesson will prove helpful and inspiring as you navigate the potential tumult. The third card reveals a pattern in your life that needs a second look. What cycle have you continuously fallen into because you have yet to resolve it? This card points to this lesson. The fourth card reveals the reward for all of your hard work during your Saturn Return. This is the cosmic treat bestowed upon you for all of your diligence! It is always nice to

have something to look forward to as you
keep your head down and do the hard work.

Uncovering your soul's purpose

Saturn represents what is important to us
based on our values, and the Saturn Return
pushes us to ascend to our highest purpose.
If you are having a hard time seeing through
the fog of confusion, try this spread – it will
allow you to uncover your core values.

   After shuffling, lay out four cards. The first
represents the answer to the question: 'Where
do my core values lay?' Look to this card to
point you in the direction of something that
is important to you. The second card answers
the question: 'What do I need to know to
assist me in following the path to my core
values?' Sometimes we need a little push or
assistance in getting to our end goal, and
this card reveals this helping hand. The third
card answers the question: 'What do I need
to know that could be an obstacle in the way

of getting to my core values?' Tarot cards do not just provide answers to our queries, but also allow us to be mindful of challenges that might get in our way so we can properly prepare ourselves. The fourth card answers the question: 'How do I apply this wisdom?' Now that you have a better understanding of your core values, this card uncovers how to apply and integrate this revelation into your life as you move forward.

Letting it go

If anything is not in alignment, the Saturn Return will confront you with the challenge of letting go of all that is no longer serving you. Change is challenging, even when it is for our greatest good, and this four-card tarot spread can help you better understand what you need to let go of in order for you to embrace change more comfortably and to do so with greater wisdom.

The first card reveals what you are having a hard time letting go of in your life. Pinpointing the challenge is always the first step! The second card shows what is stopping you from letting this element go. Having a better understanding of yourself and the obstacle can allow you to navigate this part of the cycle more clearly. The third card shows how this situation is affecting your life. Sometimes we need to be hit over the head with information in order to truly see how we are being held back by something or someone. The fourth card reveals how you can let go of this situation. This information reveals the steps you need to take in order to fully release this challenge. Creating a tangible plan of action makes the release so much easier to negotiate.

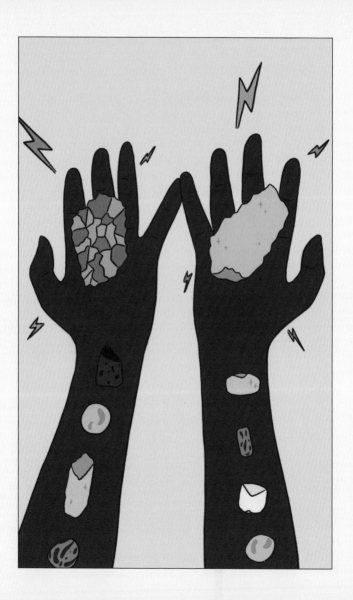

Return to Saturn:
A crystal healing meditation
– by Bri Luna

*Bri Luna is the owner and creative director
of The Hoodwitch*

Regular meditation is essential in enhancing
our intuition. It allows us the time to silence
and rest our minds in a chaotic world where
we are continuously rushed, stressed and in
a constant state of unease. The pressures of
attending school, working or parenting can be
tremendously draining, both physically and
mentally. It is essential that we take time out
of our busy schedules to focus on ourselves.

Saturn is referred to as the lord of karma.
In planetary magic, Saturn corresponds to
the day Saturday. Saturn's energy can be
helpful in times of chaos, asserting healthy
boundaries, psychic attack and protective/
defensive magic. Saturn's energy is also
best when used to bring major structure

and order into your life. In meditation,
Saturn may be called upon to reveal to you
any karmic lessons that you need to have
brought into focus.

In the mineral world, Saturn is associated
with the stones smoky quartz, jet, obsidian,
black tourmaline, tiger's eye and apache tear.
You may utilise any of these stones to place
in your hands or on your altar during your
meditation.

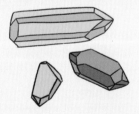

1. Select a room that is quiet and softly illuminated.

2. Your clothing should be comfortable, and shoes should not be worn.

3. Select the mineral you feel most comfortable with connecting you to Saturn.

4. Once you are seated in a comfortable position, begin a rhythmic breathing sequence by inhaling deeply through the nose, holding the breath for three seconds, and then slowly exhaling through the mouth. As you inhale, visualise cleansing white light entering your body through your nose, travelling down your trachea and filling your lungs, chest cavity and heart centre with warm, glowing sensations.

5. As you exhale, visualise any negative or lower vibrational energy, tension, confusion and stress leaving your body through your

mouth in dark, cloudy swirls of energy.
Cast these lower vibrations into the ether
to find peaceful resolution, and call in the
energy of Saturn.

6. Pick up your selected mineral/crystal with
your left hand and allow your consciousness
to merge with your crystal.

7. As you inhale, hold your crystal with
both hands. Feel the transmuted energy
peacefully flowing into your hands. Let the
crystal tell you about itself. What is your
karmic lesson, what do you need to know and
what should you be paying attention to?

8. Allow any messages, visions, words and
colours to merge into your consciousness.

9. When you feel ready to return from your
meditation, simply count backwards from ten
to one. At the count of one, open your eyes
and breathe deeply several times.

10. Remain seated and allow yourself time to reintegrate with reality. Enjoy the moments and the vibrations that fill you as you reflect on your meditation experience.

11. Place your crystal on your altar space. Make sure that your meditation crystals are cleansed upon the next use. You may need to get up and move around, allowing yourself time to journal any thoughts or symbols that presented themselves to you. If you're feeling floaty, holding a smoky quartz can also help ground you after meditation.

12. Thank Saturn for the wisdom that has been shared. Light a black candle for energetic protection and place it on your altar.

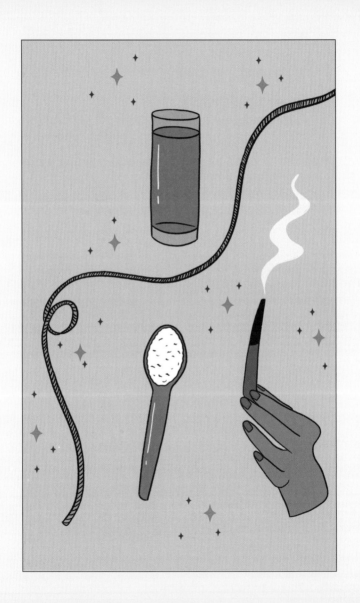

Road Opener spell
– by Christine O'Day

Christine O'Day is a magic practitioner, tarot reader, psychic and owner of The Fitness Witch (an esoteric life-coaching company)

Ingredients

- ¼ cup sea salt
- a small bowl of water
- pen and paper
- incense
- incense burner
- 4 tea light candles
- a cord in the colour of your choice

Directions

1. Begin preparing for your spell by setting aside an hour or two where you can be alone and not be disturbed. Start by taking a ritual bath in sea-salt water – this will relax

and purify the mind and body for the work ahead. Take your time to release any stress and tension from your day, and to switch your mindset from the mundane to the magical. When you feel you're finished, let the water drain out of the bath completely, envisioning all negative thoughts draining away with the water.

2. When the bath is empty, get out, dry off and continue either in the nude or in clean clothing – preferably something that makes you feel powerful. You can also wear jewellery and apply make-up. Anything that helps you tap in and makes you feel good about yourself will assist with the spellwork.

3. Get your piece of paper and a pen and write down as clearly and concisely as possible why you need roads to open. The more specific you can be, the better. Really feel the emotion of desire take over you.

4. Place the bowl of water, bowl of salt, incense and burner on the altar. Starting in the east, point your index finger at the floor and create a circle, seeing in your mind's eye bright blue flames, and saying, 'By the power of spirit do I create this circle, be thou a sphere of protection against all that is opposed to this work.' Light a candle in each quarter and, starting in the east, raise your arms to the sky and say, 'I call on the watchers of the east to witness this rite and guard this circle.' Walk to the south and say, 'I call on the watchers of the south to witness this rite and to guard this circle.' Walk to the west and say, 'I call on the watchers of the west to witness this rite and to guard this circle.' Finally, walk to the north and say, 'I call on the watchers of the north to witness this rite and to guard this circle.'

5. Go to the altar and put a pinch of salt in the water, then walk clockwise around the circle and say, 'I cleanse this circle by water and earth', then light some incense and, again, walk around the circle and say, 'I purify this circle by fire and air.' Return to the altar and say, 'In the name of the Goddess and God, so mote it be!'

6. Return to the altar and read aloud your intention to the energies you have called to aid you. Then pick up your cord. Starting at one end, tie a knot and say, 'By knot of one, the spell's begun.' Now tie another knot at the other end and say, 'By knot of two, this spell comes true.' Tie a knot next to the first and say, 'By knot of three, this spell shall be.' Tie the fourth next to the second and say, 'By knot of four, I open this door.' Tie the fifth knot next to the third and say, 'By knot of five, this spell is alive!' Tie the sixth next to the fourth and say, 'By knot of six, this spell is fixed!'

Tie the seventh next to the fifth and say, 'By knot of seven, link earth to heaven.' Tie the eighth next to the sixth and say, 'By knot of eight, this seals my fate.' Then tie the ninth in the centre and say, 'By knot of nine, this spell doth bind!'

7. Now that your ritual is complete, address each quarter, as before, starting in the east, this time saying, 'I bid ye farewell watchers of the east, thank you for your presence, may you depart in peace.'

8. Walk counter clockwise, pointing an index finger at the floor, imagining the blue flames dissolving, and say, 'This circle has ended, yet it ever remains a circle, around and through me always flows its magical power. So mote it be.'

Saturn Return manifestation – by Renee Watt

Renee Watt is a tarot reader, witch, psychic and host of the Witch Doctorate podcast

Saturn Returns can be painful. The universe asks you to take a look at the things that are no longer working for you, so you can make changes and evolve as a human. One of the more difficult aspects of this time period is identifying toxic friendships and relationships. Partnerships of all varieties are likely to shift, and taking the time to identify who has your best interests at heart will help you decide who should stay in your sphere and who it's better to let go of.

One thing that will help you identify toxicity is by paying attention to who creates drama in your life. If you've got a friend who seems to create problems or find reasons to trigger conflict (either with them or between you and other people), it may be time to re-evaluate your connection to that person. Additionally, if you find that you're an emotional support for someone but they're not there for you, it might be time to move on. Take some time to think these relationships over, and try to communicate your concerns before resorting to any sort of ritual. By attempting to hold a conversation, you'll allow these people to evolve as you transform your personal relationships with them. If you find that conversation is ineffective, I recommend trying a banishing ritual.

Whenever I'm working to banish a person from my life, I will usually banish the unhealthy energy they bring into my space, rather than casting on the actual person. This again provides an opportunity for growth. However, in many cases people do not change. For this reason, before performing my ritual I make peace with the fact that by banishing these behaviours, I may be banishing the person as well.

This spell is best performed during a full moon, and you will need the following items:

- a piece of paper and pen
- a black chime candle and holder
- a small plate or piece of foil (to catch wax from your candle)
- a small bowl of salt water (you can collect this from the sea, or make your own by dissolving a teaspoon of sea salt in ¼ cup of distilled water).

Before you begin, take a moment to write down all of the drama, habits or conflict you wish to rid your life of. You'll want to begin the list with the phrase: 'I banish ...' What you write down can be specific to a person (i.e. 'I banish Karen's drama'), or more general (i.e. 'I banish being taken advantage of').

Once you have your list complete, hold it in your hand while visualising these problems melting away from your life. Allow your thoughts to marinate for a bit as you sit in silence. When you feel ready, say the following:

'I call on the universe (or your higher power) to hear this petition.'

Then read your list out loud. (Be sure to say 'I banish' at the beginning of your list and before you read each item.)

Next, take your list and place it face down under your foil or plate, then place your candle on top. Make sure your dish of salt water is within a few centimetres of this set-up as well. Finally, light your candle while saying:

'So be it.'

Take a moment of quiet and thank the universe (or your higher power) for working with you.

Allow your candle to burn to completion and leave your spell materials where they are overnight. The next day, you'll want to bury your candle and list outside. Once you've completed this task, pour the salt water over the dirt.

Now that you've done some work to remove toxic energy from your life, perform a follow-up ritual to call in some good. This spell is very similar to the banishing ritual mentioned above, with a few variations.

It is best to perform this spell during a new moon. You will need the following items:

- a piece of paper and pen
- a white chime candle and holder
- a small plate or piece of foil (to catch wax from your candle)
- a small bowl of milk mixed with honey, or almond milk with agave

This spell is focused towards inviting positive people, opportunities or habits into your life. Think about healthy and uplifting things you want to enjoy more, and write them down on your paper. As you make your list, begin by writing down 'I bring in' and then notate what it is you're calling on (i.e. job growth, supportive friendships, a supportive partner, confidence). Once you've finished, hold the list up to your heart for a moment, close your eyes and take deep breaths, allowing positive feelings to fill your heart and aura. Imagine yourself surrounded by love, and try to send love out to the universe. Once you're ready, say the following:

'I call upon the universe (or your higher power) to hear this petition.'

Then read your words out loud. (Don't forget to state that you wish to call in the things noted on your list.)

Next, take your list and place it face up under your foil or plate, then place your candle on top. Make sure your dish of milk and honey is within a few centimetres of this set-up as well. Finally, light your candle while saying:

'So be it.'

Take a moment of quiet and thank the universe (or your higher power) for working with you.

As with the banishing ritual, allow your candle to burn to completion and leave your spell materials where they are overnight. The next day, bury your candle and list outside. Take a moment to thank the universe once again, and then pour the milk over the burial site.

Your intentions may vary as your life evolves, but you can perform these spells each month, or whenever you feel drawn to to this. Happy manifesting!

'I THINK YOU HAVE
DIFFERENT SOULMATES
THROUGHOUT YOUR LIFE,
THAT YOUR SOUL NEEDS
DIFFERENT THINGS AT
DIFFERENT TIMES.
I DO BELIEVE IN LOVE.
I WILL ALWAYS BELIEVE IN
LOVE, BUT MY IDEA HAS
CHANGED FROM WHAT
I'VE ALWAYS THOUGHT.'

– KIM KARDASHIAN WEST

CHAPTER 8

CONCLUSION

Saturn is the teacher who wants you to pass their class ... but only if you've done all your homework and aced the exam. If you don't, you fail. You won't get praise for what you've done right. Saturn's mission is to point out what's not working and why. (Sorry, but you don't make the rules – your fate and the cosmos do.)

Because your Saturn Return only lasts two to three years, ask yourself what you want to accomplish in that time. Then, start making moves. Luckily, no matter how difficult it may be to take a brutally honest look at your life, you have the chance – at this astrological point – to turn things around. You might not get that opportunity again, so roll up those metaphorical sleeves and take your Saturn Return seriously. Yes, it may take work, struggle or sacrifice. After

all, success requires you to push yourself
beyond your comfort zone, and that's what
Saturn does. Exactly which comfort zone
that is depends on you. Your Saturn Return
can manifest itself in a tonne of different
ways, from a demanding task that you must
accomplish to a person who enlightens you.
However the ringed planet shows up in your
life, you'll emerge from the experience wiser
and more capable of achieving whatever it
is your soul desires. Ultimately, if you listen
and learn from Saturn, you will begin to see
it for what it is –your best friend. Even if you
don't believe in the Saturn Return, or any
cosmic intervention for that matter, guess
what? Nothing bad can happen as a result
of quitting behaviours that aren't serving you
and intentionally chasing your goals.
If you've been there and made it out the other
side, then you know. If you're yet to turn
30, you may still have a potential pre-thirty
freak-out in your late twenties to look forward

to (you lucky thing). But take the lessons Saturn is throwing your way as celestial growing pains – they may be hard, messy, awkward and bizarre at times, but they're well worth the drama and the roller-coaster ride, because you will grow, evolve, and never be the same.

Bring it on, Saturn! We're ready!

EVERYTHING WE THINK ACTUALLY MATTERS. IF WE ARE SEEKING SUCCESS, WE MUST THINK SUCCESSFUL, INSPIRING AND MOTIVATING THOUGHTS.

GLOSSARY

air signs: these are the signs of Gemini, Libra and Aquarius. They are the intellectuals and thinkers of the zodiac.

ascendant (ASC): also known as the rising sign. This is the sign on the cusp of the first house of the birth chart. It is the sign, and degree of that sign, that is rising on the eastern horizon at the moment of birth, in relation to the place of birth.

aspects: aspects are an important part of modern astrology. As the planets move in their elongated orbits around the Sun, they form various angular relationships with one another, using the Sun or Earth as the centre. These are called aspects. The most popular aspects result from dividing the circle by numbers like 1, 2, 3 or 4, resulting in aspects such as the conjunction (0 degrees), opposition (180 degrees), trine (120 degrees), square (90 degrees), and so forth.

When two planets form an aspect with one another, their energies and natures are said to combine and work either in harmony or in discord. For example, when two planets are exactly on opposite sides of the Sun (Earth), they are in opposition.

birth chart: drawn for a person's birth; also known as a natal chart. The birth chart is a map of one's life. Like taking a picture of the planets at the time of one's birth, it shows the universe, stopped at that moment in time, and reveals what the universe has to say about who a person is and what they may become. The chart wheel is a map of the space surrounding a person at the time of birth. The wheel is divided into 12 sections called houses. Planets in the heavens are placed on the chart wheel in the houses that correspond to where they actually are in the sky at birth.

cardinal signs: these are the signs of Aries, Cancer, Libra and Capricorn, and are related to the change of the seasons.

earth signs: these are the signs of Taurus, Virgo and Capricorn.

fire signs: these are the signs of Aries, Leo and Sagittarius.

fixed signs: these are the signs of Taurus, Leo, Scorpio and Aquarius.

hard aspects: generally considered the conjunction, opposition and square. In midpoint work, the hard aspects also include the semi-square and sesquiquadrate. These represent challenge, obstacles and substance. They provide meat and potatoes in our life. Too many can block or obstruct the life flow, yet too few can cause life to be weak or thin.

houses: the horoscope divides the heavens into 12 houses. Each house has rulership over specific areas of life.

orb: when determining whether one planet forms an aspect to another, astrologers allow an 'orb' of influence, which is a specific number of degrees. Aspects between planets gradually form, become exact and separate. When an aspect is exact, it has its greatest impact. Yet, the effect of most aspects can be felt for some time before and after the moment when it is exact.

The range within which an aspect is in operation is called its 'orb of influence', or simply its orb. An orb of one or two degrees of arc on either side of the exact aspect is considered a close or tight orb, while an orb of 10 degrees is loose.

planetary rulers: each sign is ruled by a planet. See our planetary rulers page for more information.

retrograde: a planet is considered 'retrograde' when it appears to be moving backwards. Both 'retrograde' and 'direct' are terms used in astrology to describe the direction of planetary movement with relation to the Earth. Note that the planets do not actually move backwards. However, they appear (from our perspective on Earth) to back up for periods of time. The Sun and the Moon never retrograde.

water signs: these are the signs of Cancer, Scorpio and Pisces.

zodiac: a circle of 360 degrees, divided into 12 equal sectors of 30 degrees each that comprise the astrology signs.

Acknowledgements

It takes a village to raise a child, even after their Saturn Return. I would like to thank the following people for their personal and professional support throughout the years.

Special shout out to Bri Luna, Christine O'Day, Sarah Potter and Renee Watt for their magical and inspiring contributions to this book.

To Mom, Dad, Jessica, Nate, Avery, Riley, AC, Grandma Anne, Grandpa Gene, Oma, Grandpa Norbert, Jonathan, Aunt Linda, Uncle Marc, Uncle Danny, Molly, Randi, Paige, Ilene, Dominick Travis, Samantha Baker, Spencer Baker, Tara Foster, Annabel Gat, Anne Ortelee, Sonia Ortiz, Blue June, Michael Cardenas, Kesaine Walker, Rachel True, Liz Goldwyn, Adam Cerny, Lexi Ferguson, Heather Breen, Caitlin McGarry, Arseny Libon, Jessica Lanyadoo, Nancy Hayes, Kristy Belich, Nina Kahn, Kyle Thomas, Maia Lorian, Six, Danny Larkin, Narayana Montúfar, Stephanie Powell, Didi Daze, Kawano-Sensei, Gabrielle Gottlieb, Lindsay Peoples Wagner, Brittney McNamara, Emily Shippee, Samhita Mukhopadhyay, Tahira Hairston, Dani Kwateng-Clark, Asia Milia Ware, Arianna Davis, Elena Nicolaou, Erika Smith, Jenni Miller, Jen Ortiz, Rachel Torgerson, Mia Lardiere, Sara Radin, Kayla Greeves, Kristin Magaldi, Allison Ives, Jerico Mandybur, Sara Tardiff, Emily Dufton, Markeeta Waddington, Mirel Zaman, Karina Hoshikawa, Elizabeth Gulino, Elena Nicolaou, Mirel Zaman, Alison Ives, Samantha Sutton, Kylie Gilbert and Elisabeth Krohn. Last but definitely not least, my wonderful and encouraging editor Alice Hardie-Grant for her patience and dedication to this project. And, Emmy Lupin for creating all of the beautiful art for this book.

Published in 2021 by Hardie Grant Books,
an imprint of Hardie Grant Publishing

Hardie Grant Books (Melbourne)
Building 1, 658 Church Street
Richmond, Victoria 3121

Hardie Grant Books (London)
5th & 6th Floors
52–54 Southwark Street
London SE1 1UN

hardiegrantbooks.com

Commissioning Editor: Alice Hardie-Grant
Editor: Vanessa Lanaway
Design Manager: Mietta Yans
Cover design: Lila Theodoros
Layout design: Mietta Yans
Production Manager: Todd Rechner

Colour reproduction by Splitting Image
Colour Studio
Printed in China by Leo Paper Products LTD.

Hardie Grant acknowledges the
Traditional Owners of the country on
which we work, the Wurundjeri people of
the Kulin nation and the Gadigal people
of the Eora nation, and recognises their
continuing connection to the land, waters
and culture. We pay our respects to their
Elders past, present and emerging.

The paper this book is printed on is
from FSC®-certified forests and other
sources. FSC® promotes environmentally
responsible, socially beneficial and
economically viable management of the
world's forests.

A catalogue record for this
book is available from the
National Library of Australia

Saturn Return Survival Guide
ISBN 9781743796641

10 9 8 7 6 5 4 3 2 1

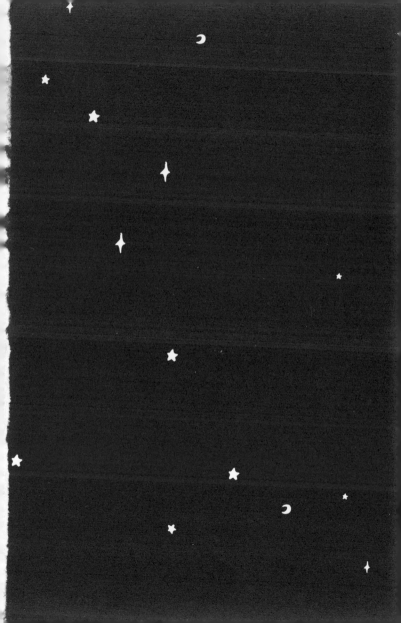